Smoking in Mom's Garage

To James,

in friendship.
and admiration.

Nancy Patrice Davenport

poems by **Nancy Patrice Davenport**

Red Alice's Books 2018

Acknowledgements –
Various forms of some of these poems
have previously appeared in:

Allegro & Adagio: Dance Poems,
Blue Fifth Review, Country Valley Press,
Crazy Child Scribbler, Empty Hands Broadside #23,
Full of Crow, Haight Ashbury Literary Journal,
I Am Not a Silent Poet, It Happened Under Cover,
La Brizna: Bookgirl Press, Mountains and Rivers Press,
Naked Bulb Anthology 2017, Poetry Quarterly,
Red Fez, Rose Red Review, The Lake, The Rag #7,
The Szygy Poetry Journal No. 4, The Tarot Poetry Anthology,
Twisted Tungz Anniversary Issue

For continued influence, special appreciation to:

Robert Hunter, e. e. cummings,
Cid Corman, Charlie Merhoff,
Lorine Niedecker

Special thank you to: Evan Myquest

Front cover photo by Zoe Christopher
Cover design by Red Alice Books

Red Alice Books
P.O. Box 262, Penn Valley, CA 95946
U.S.A.

ISBN: 978-0-9971780-4-3
Library of Congress Control Number: 2018938104

for

Lorin Krogh and Sally A. Davenport.

Contents –

Introduction by Paul Corman-Roberts

Introduction

Davenport is very much her own poet. She is that throwback who holds her conversation on the medium of the page where she is indeed conversing, not inventing, not hiding, and not playing word games. Yet, despite her laid back groove, Davenport is unquestionably an original. By the time the reader reaches the end of one of her poems, the senses will have been expanded, and the mind given no choice but to follow.

In the very highest sense of the word, Davenport's poems can be called poems of recovery; recovery of the self, recovery of the page, recovery of sensual sensibility and yes, recovery of the poem itself. If you want to know why poetry endures, turn the following pages and embrace the collective remembrance of a poet who refused to fall into the cracks of the 21st century's hype –

Paul Corman-Roberts

Smoking in Mom's Garage

JUNE TWILIGHT ALPHAS #2

At the beginning, my poems had nothing to do with me, almost all of them. As my life has gone on, one thing I've said is I began writing fully clothed and I took off my clothes bit by bit. Now I'm writing naked.

— *Donald Hall*

an oriole   sings

the world as I
know it

turns off

a warm night
made for

nightgown
and notebook

dad's old red   Peruvian   poncho
while the light of the
Friday 13 full moon
fills the entire back
yard with   a surrealistic
color

I strip and
write a poem

WINDOW DRESSING

after that kiss

I shut the
front door

see him dance
a soft shoe
outside

in the long lights
of the setting
sun

THE SAVAGE

you thought
you had
yourself

               a lady
white gloves
basket purse
and pearls

but naked

you find yourself
with a peasant

hairy un-plucked unshaken
both feet on the floor
lips   open

my mother disliked   douches
dyes   depilatories

I belong to the ages

I will shine like fire
humid   dripping
as furry and sweet

as a peach

finger licking good

but afterward

you may find yourself
sheets pulled
up
with a lady

HOMESICK #2

so tired from
insomnia
but not numb
enough to
stop counting
the hours

till I get back to what is what

I am not a traveler

but an explorer

there is a difference

the ocean roars in my ears

it is easy enough to sit down
with a book
fiddle away
the hours

but only when my sister's
tom with one eye blind

that looks like a jewel from
the bottom of the sea

like a pirate's treasure
           booty
jumps on my bed
am I able to take
a deep breath

and relax

because you are here too

POWER OUTAGE

there is a ghost
a symphony
in my drapes tonight

I can hear a loon's
silent song

along with the beginning strains
of *O, What a Lovely War*

while I read *Gatsby*
in the dark

my dog is back
to fetch
his phantom ball

the drapes are my mom's
maxi skirt from 1972

when she first
found herself

alone in this living room
asking questions

watching the drapes
dance in the wind

during another power outage

SKUNK IN FALL #4

albino skunk

like Alfred E. Neuman

like Lyndon B. Johnson

like the Buddha

WITH INSPIRATION
FROM GROUP THERAPY

there is a galaxy of cobwebs
on the patio
in the sunlight
this morning

formless reflections   of light
       life
dark   star   crashing

an entire new world
underneath
a tile

electricity shooting   seeds

sometimes
starting
over is not too onerous

POEM FOR MY BIG SISTER

it's the time of year
I could follow you around,

find you

by peel,
    (by following your sweet smell)

grape cluster scaffoldings
    peach pits left on windowsills

the glove of a banana
    left on your dash,

apple core
in
ash tray

a trail
    of
cherry   pits

FORETASTE

I thought I was too old
to feel such
anticipation at prospects
desire at anticipation

oh this is grand

to wake up and notice first
thing   the sound

of finches
peeping
the California Valley Quail   singing

the color of
azaleas pushing
against mom's
picture
window

French lingerie
the smell   of my neighbor's   Daphne

I'm a patient person
but I'm impatient

for a taste
            for   foretaste
these butterflies
in my stomach
if released

would be every
color of
the rainbow

MARY TYLER MOORE
MINDFULNESS TURN-ON POEM

so   it has been one of those
times   rare and true   wonderful
when the world
is turned on
by my smile
by the gold   floating in   the air   around me

or is it just
        the world spinning a bit   faster?

it's not just your body
I want to
climb   onto

I'd   like to

climb into   it
        jump   your   bones

first,   I want to savor the   sweetness
the flavor of your mouth

your   teeth

I want   to taste   your back

your brain

find out   your favorites
your signs: astrological and Chinese

your favorite
foreign
food

listen to you   ramble

understand your

reasoning

I want to make you   belly laugh

lick   your belly

get name cones at Foster's   and find out   new
names

lick the chocolate
from
your fingers

BIRTHDAY MINDFULNESS POEM

mistakes are the portals for discovery
– James Joyce

I have always liked birthdays
cake   and opening   presents
          blowing

have never really
minded
getting older
wisdom gained painfully
          or   cheerfully

I have finally accepted the powerlessness
                    of it all

It is possible to age
backwards

while   watching   a lily   a pink lily

          bloom   petal
                    by petal.

my face   is lined with   experience
foresight   and   a few   mistakes

it's turned up to
the sun
during meditation
          for some peace

for gratitude
in love
to the warm
          morning light

I like my   grey hairs
                up and down

I   have   earned them.

I never noticed
before
the steam rising   or is   it
simply   effervescence?

BIRTHDAY MINDFULNESS POEM #2

so: not caring as the cool night

melts into morning

I think   about   redemption   about
    change

facing this   pink and yellow and grey   Crayola dawn

I find that
transformation is

a   motivational   force   when   celebrated

my self-improvement
is profound, valid
a compassion I can hold   with both hands
an insight:

the ability to laugh at me
when I look
at myself
from the   outside
I am
not so   bad
like WCW, I   sing   softly   to   myself
admire
my nakedness   my   individuality
and dance
empowered

EARTHLY COSMOS

Did you know
there is
a constellation   on   your   back?

I can't
read   stars
but   there is   handwriting
on   the   warm wall
your spine
in the   white light   of
the moon

TATTOOS

it's been   a long time
since   I have seen
you
naked

so   I   didn't know about
the tattoos
you have
added

they remind me
of a time

when   I could identify 1964   Mustangs   Cougars
        and Firebirds
each year of
Harley

when I
would   ride without a   helmet
        or leather

powerful
               without fear

but honest   I can't help it
my first thought
is how
pretty
your body looks
how much I want to touch each tattoo
without
fear

right   now

PEACOCK FEATHER EARRINGS

I have these
    hanging
        peacock
    feather earrings

the groovy hippy lady
told me
they were bad luck

but the iridescence   of them the green beauty
says something
else

there's a life energy   I   can feel
    not only from them
from the peacock
    an earth energy   a *Hado*
affecting my
physical
manifestations   a certain   power
a charm   a glamour   an allure

as you

take that earring out of my ear

and run it

up and down

my body

BARBA AMOR

woke up this morning and I got myself a beard.
- Jim Morrison

how nice it would be
to ride
in your beard
for a day to feel the muscles   better and nerves more
the shocking fuzz
as you
speak
to the   multitude
of people
you greet   during the course of your day

how nifty
it would
be to
sit   in the
sweet
curve   of your lips   and settle there, tasting
watching your
expression
change

I could carefully
walk over

the planes   of your face

get a real
good look   at the color of your eyes   finally
kiss that hair that grows
all over the side
of your face
burn   your   face   sides   with   my   tongue
again and again   and   again
slowly   stroking
the

18

electric fur, and what-is-it   comes
over parting flesh
as   you   smile
and the   resultant   explosion   of gold
dust
you   would

not even
know

I was   there

RED BRICKS

doing my number
          watering
and weeding
in my   cool   garden

sipping   sweet
coffee
at dawn   I can still   see
the new   Libra moon

reminding me
to
slow   down
          pause

think   before I act

spread   some seeds
          some beauty in my life
          in your life   his   life
our life   harvest

I put
my forehead
to the cool
brick   wall   and   pause

I can   feel your breath

on the back
of my
neck
as   the   red   bricks get   warm

OFF-MOTHER'S DAY MINDFULNESS

Peeling off   the
undershirt
I have
been wearing
for a couple of days   in my   sick and sad   haze

I   can smell you

there you
are
again
mom

PENINSULA WINTER

comes   on
         quick
after
Thanksgiving
usually   after   a few   good rains

each sidewalk
takes on the
pattern
of the   tree   above it
one or two trees   turn bright red

I become   the child
I never was
plowing   my way through
darker   Diebenkorn   colors
in old Birkenstocks

and the gone silk oak
in   mom's
back yard   fills it
with   invisible   ghostly
yellow leaves

VENUS OF DAVENPORT

the rain has
            softened me

made me
more

lush

bosomy

made	me		a bit	more	*zaftig*
my skin	is a	sort of		clay	an earth
made	of wet				
ashes		dust	and	remains	
moist					

waiting for you
waiting for your   touch

waiting for your   fingerprints

not so much
fascinated
by how

as by   when

THE CHEVY

we ride   in   Dad's   basket-colored 1957
Chevy
sedan
sitting in   the   double-row   of seats
like   newly-hatched   baby birds
peeping

daddy   with   one arm out the window 180°
has   his   black   Ray-Bans
mom   is   smiling   a pony-tailed   chick   with her
smart
scarf tied
around
her head
big   round   dark   glasses
which to us
seems   perfect
watching the
road
pass through
holes
in the floor   of the old   Chevy
until   the   divorce

ANGELS AUF HIMMEL

the cover said:
> *Angels auf Himmel*
> with   a black
and white
photograph of
a couple   of   buxom   women
that didn't
look
American

I remember
finding

it under the old   green   couch
with
Grandma Davenport
when we
were
moving

I was   a bit   embarrassed
did it belong
to my   dad
to my
brother   or   even   my   female cousin?
but
Grandma   smiled
said:

look Anna
the brown   haired   girl
she is so sweet
she looks   like you

TRIUMPHUS

In my   dream
I
laugh
in
the guest room   across the   hall
that she has
set up
with the funny   sweet-smelling
feather   bed

naked
counting each   tattoo on
her   blonde tanned body

as the smell of
winter
Daphne

comes   in
   through an   open   window

WRITER'S BLOCK POEM

I think the highest and lowest points are the important ones.
Anything else is just...in between.

— Jim Morrison

I   am   blocked
unable to
write   one   damn   decent word
the most beautiful   thing   I can
manage
is   the   arc   my   crumpled   up
poem
makes
as   I   throw   it
into
the
growing   pile   in   my old

Spider-Man
garbage
can

SHE RISES

drums
dreams
I   come
naked
born   engendered
from   the   rib   of   Mother   Earth
covered with
ash and
mud
wicker and
dead   leaves
steam   and   smoke
mist   rain   fog
I   will   rise/emerge
when   I
touch   you
I will   leave   smears of

blood
dirt
blue paint

MOCHA MEETING DAYDREAM

before   dinner   and   meeting

with my ex

I asked
to
stop   at Peet's

and

instead   of   my   usual   large   drip
with lots-of-room-for-cream
I chose a   chocolate   mocha
I think this may be because
this
hot   whip-cream   topped   deliciousness
deep   dark   liquid   thick
both   hands on   the   cup
sipped   slow
to   make   it   last
reminds me   mmm
of   you

FRIDAY NIGHT IN MOM'S GARAGE
MINDFULNESS

so,

                    I am
smoking in my   pajamas
in   mom's garage
the smoke   shivers
with me
oak trees   have   green   tips

El Niño   pounds
on the shake   roof
and the   albino skunk
appears   at   the   screen door
looks   in
and walks
away

MORNING SWEEP

this   morning

I found mom's
old   wood
broom in
the
garage
funny how   good   it still   works

I tied   my   hair   in   a scarf
and
went to work

found the   old   bent
dustpan

hanging   on the wall
took   that   broom to   my   life
first   my   expectations

I cleaned those up first

TERRAPIN POEM (POEM FOR LORIN) #2

watching   the   birds   fly   in cursive
circles   over
the bay

I think of you
your   free-for-alls on land
to take   each   step
on this earth

you remind me of   a turtle
hard-backed out of necessity
from steps and scars
but very soft underneath
when one took the time
to turn you over

I see you
walking slowly   towards a   low   tide
with acceptance
without   gravity   free
flying
soaring

RESPONSE VS REACTION

you know,
you aren't allowed to miss me

do you think you have   fooled me?

I could smell you   from   across
the room

see you
        taking your steps a bit too   carefully

I wasn't trying to watch.   Do
you   think   I wanted   to   see   this?

I will not miss   you

will put your bracelet
in the box

do you understand   you have become
                        unrecognizable?
a squatter   no longer   yourself?
if I turn the other cheek   again
my head is going to   fly the fuck off

You are not allowed to miss me who are you?
I will not miss   you
I won't let you piss me off   asshole
you don't deserve
my emotion
are not worthy
of my divine shaking   rage

INSIGNIFICANCY MINDFULNESS POEM

*Do not be afraid, our fate cannot be
taken from us; it is a gift*
                                    Dante

I am sand

I am snow
the top of
water
written on,   rewritten, erased   by time

I have led a sheltered life

invisible in the front of rooms
a space that defines itself
by not being and being
there

untouchable   bottom feeder

I have such a good
smile
but I can't   always
stand behind it

nothing can   get   at me

I can get at
        nothing

bodiless   a   voice   heard   not heard

nothing
nichts
nada
boo
diddley-squat
fuck-all
but

I think you   might

miss me if   I   weren't   here

HAND MINDFULNESS POEM

my hand rolls   the   dice

it   walks
with   each   finger

my hand
is a
clenched fist

my hand
has
eyes
in the back of its   head

my hands
are
geishas

they hold
you

soft gently with warm   mouth licks

my hand
has
bitten
nails

sharp   and   scratchy

my hand
is
a
flirt

my hand is
a burning
bush

my hands   are   sobbing

they create a   warm   river

my hand has
phantom
fingers

like the sunset

one hand
is a
skunk
quiet   roaming   peaceful
              stinky   when   pissed

the other
hand

a   lone   wolf
howling

my hands
Picasso
paintings

imperfect
perfect

my hand
is

feathered   and   flies

my hands
are

always open

BEDROOM MINDFULNESS SONG

my   bedroom
is   an   odd   shape

made for
naps   and   antique furniture
for   sweet   sweaty sex
            in the afternoons

for   bong   hits
one window   allows in the dawn
            the other

faces the night stars

it's as if
the
Oakland   designer   fiddled

until   it was   imperfect

BEDROOM MINDFULNESS SONG #2

it's   a   trapezium:
a turn-on
floors   precipitous   and   un-level
the   perfectly-shaped   rectangle   windows
flood my very white flesh
color it
meld it   with
my   lover's stained-glass   story   book   skin
there are stars stars   too   many   to   count
five-pointed
on the   ceiling
left over
from the person   who   lived
here before
me

ONE IN A SERIES OF MINDFUL
POCKET LOVE POEMS

it's effortless:
a mutually   intense
vigorous physical   struggle

bodies   taking   to it
just   like   that

with   immediacy   and   horsepower
we   are

in the
pink

SLEEP/LOVE MINDFULNESS POEM

I like watching people   sleep

my big sister
crowding into
my twin
bed with me

when   I   was   small

perhaps it's
because I've
never been able
to sleep myself

the voices in my head keeping me   awake
one way or another
but this isn't always so bad
there's a security in hearing/seeing/knowing
a cat curling into a C
Little Dog's sweet pepper perfume

my brother's snores
through the wall

my grandmother's favorite blue flower closing
at the end of the day

there   is something about   knowing that   other
creatures
are   asleep
that
says   everything
is going to be all right
for   now

I love   watching you   sleep
after   we   fuck
while   the   glow   is   still   around
my   thighs   trembling

I climb   into the colors   of your chest and tell   myself
epic love stories
of what   will   be

watch   the   thump   of   your   heartbeat through
your   chest

count   each   body   hair

smell   your   beard

listen   to
you
breathe

SLEEP/LOVE MINDFULNESS POEM #2

another   rainy   morning
and   I'm   taking
my mood
out
on   my   lover
         slamming   doors

snapping at   this   and   that

let's go back to yesterday

when the rain   first   started
grey   dark
he took me   back   to   bed
in the middle of the day

exposing the   first   band   of   color
in   the   sky   and
on his   body   rainbows
rainbows
as the   sun   went   down
how   does a   leopard change her   spots?
by moving   from   place   to   place

SON IN TOWN MINDFULNESS POEM

my son is here
I've made him a room
in the
house in Oakland
put his A on the wall

we are   getting
accustomed
to each   other   again

I listen for   the   sound of   his   breathing
when he is asleep

do his laundry

he gets   familiar
with my habits   silence   headphones
and   bong-hits

we move in turn with each other

off-mirror images

funny

some   things   never   change
the smell of his shit

still   does   not
bother
me

CHRISTMAS PRESENT OAKLAND
MINDFULNESS POEM

Welcome Winter Solstice, in our hearts we burn warm   grateful
with all that you offer

all we hold dear

the tree has been decorated

in your
honor

my soul is a little more
invigorated
now

my pen is flying
I am eating the richer foods

my   lover   is
cooking

my son
is here

under my
wing

mom's candlesticks   out   and   lit
my   grandmother's candy dish full
this is to   me   comfort and   joy

the windowpanes
can rattle
as

much   as   they   wish

baby,   it might be   cold   outside
but it's warm in here
our haven
safe   safe
the beauty   and   significance
of winter
simply cannot be overlooked

CHRISTMAS PRESENT OAKLAND
MINDFULNESS POEM #2

another Christmas   Eve

the   dawn   stars
this morning have me   thinking
of   old   times

hard-up years

black-out years not so   ho-ho-ho

my son   when   he   was   four   months   old

mom's birthday on the 17th
cancer in remission

that   year   we   celebrated   on Boxer   Day
because

you decided to bring a bottle
on
Christmas   and   barfed –

my   lost   moonstone   ring

the   year   after   mom   when
nobody
gave   me   anything

as   I   stare   at   the   morning   stars
and
smoke

I   can't   help   but   think

funny how   now   through the   course of   time

these   hard   times

have   been   manifested

as   good   times

SWIFFER OAKLAND MINDFULNESS POEM

the not-level hardwood   floors
of
this old   house

a constant
attraction for dirt and grime

little tornadoes begin
when the heater
comes on

a dust bunny trembles in each corner
waiting for
my touch

Swiffer standing in the kitchen
is giving
me the eye
telling me to get to work

but the   effect of   dust   dancing on   sunlight
has always
been

for me   soporific

doubly so when I am   listening to RIPPLE
and singing   along

so I leave
the derechos
and dust bunnies
and the   gold   dust   alone

smash   my   face
against
a beam of light

and put my
Swiffer
away

OAKLAND EPILEPSY SIREN SONG #2

the   linkage   from
my
brain   to   my   body

can   be   a   delicate mechanism

often now

broken   and   uncoupled

after   I   find   myself
among

the   dust   bunnies again

I must   wait
stop

make   basic   decisions
about   what   it is

I am   trying
to
do

until   slowly

the

basic rhythm   is   reestablished

OAKLAND TAROT LOVE POEM

there really is something
special
about

this

you a joker
in a Tarot deck

while   I   am   the   card
with the old rules for playing

it's not just
the colorful semantic
connection of

your home town
and
my last name

you   are

a silver surfer

noble and tormented by life
but
you have   saved   me   from   the   drab
world of my existence

OAKLAND SILENCE MINDFULNESS POEM

after   midnight

moon   haloed   by   rainbow

Oakland   noise   becomes different
special
something   undefinable
the smoke from   my   cigarette speaks to   me
in
   swirling-swirls

as my   brain   talks

bus   stops   arriving

a Lake   Merritt goose   flies   by   making no
   noise
the crow   on   the   line as still   as   mouse

rain   drops   one   by   one

stars   shimmer

and the black cat from across
the street

stares   at   me

listening   to   the   silence   too

EPILEPSY SIREN SONG #7

good morning   dust

nice to see
you
again

down   here among   the motey   motes

pinned
to

the day   to   the   rag rug
like a   bug

powerless

but not   so   bad   really

I   am   here
where
the
sun falls   warm
complete with   gold   dust

the colors of the rag rug   are a   lot   brighter

and if I move

just   a   little

a   beam   of   the   sun's   light

hits me

square   in   the   face

VIRGO-PISCES LOVE SONG

I like this new love

we
so different
but
so
damn similar

I'm not   sure how two   people who   look

so different from
each other

can   be   cut   from   the   same   cloth

no roller coasters here
we   don't   play   Risk   or   Monopoly

a few   butterflies   when   you come
in every   color

we don't really disagree

oh we   fight   now   and then
raise   hell   on   earth

fireworks

then come back together
like   rain   to   earth
like   bees   to   honey
like   the   ocean   to   the   shore

steady

it's   so   damn   easy   to   breathe
to laugh

steady
like   a   healthy   heart   beat

PARKING LOT MINDFULNESS SONG

in   the   Safeway   parking lot
two geese go by

honk   honk
honk   honk

all of us waiting   outside
suddenly
become
friends
grinning   at   each   other

"where's the horn?"

one   smiley   man
asks
me

I   give him a smoke
and   give   another   smoke
and   my   pocket full   of
change   to
the   lady
who   has   her   very   own   cart

58

OAKLAND LOVE POEM

it   is   rather   beautiful

my knees
have

a way of trembling

when   my   body   is   very   happy

their   way
of   saying   thank you
to
Gabriel   head   back

who has made them sing

sing in the   silver-green   Oakland   rain

big and
small

diamonds   that   drop on
my old
roof

rest

on the   trees
and

the   pink   rosebush   outside

OAKLAND RAIN SONG #2

it's almost   Halloween

drizzly

and I   can't   afford
my
meds   until   my   check   comes

living on coffee   and editing

and sweet   Jesus

the voices
I take

the meds for are beginning to chatter

chatter   even   howl

all of   them   male female

ghosts are here

shadow   hands licking   at   me

telling me
to be

the old   me

the can't-be
the burn-me
the cut-me

double vision   makes   even

doing   nothing   fucking   hard

but moth   in   a   jar

there   is   no   way   out

of   the   empty   med   bottle

HENDRIX DAWN MINDFULNESS POEM

there's   a   bright   purple   haze
over   Oakland
this   morning

my   fingernails   have   grown   out   long   and
          lovely I see

funny thing
when they   are   bitten
my   hands   look   like   dad's

when my nails are long like   this
my   hands   are like mom's

I   never   thought I would be like my parents
both   calm   as   the   water   I've   put   in
the bottom   part of the scarlet   begonia pot
there's   mom
and   murky   salty   and   deep   dark   like   Lake
          Merritt
there's   dad

fist   dad
palm   mom

all   this   thinking
while the haze   in the sky has turned a bit darker purple

will   you   excuse   me   mom   and   dad
while I   kiss   it?

DECEMBER MINDFULNESS POEM #3

my   boy   is   awake

I   can   hear
him

playing   jazz   in   the   shower

clearing   his   throat

he sounds   like   me

like   my   mother

it's   interesting   how   everything
looks

so   much   more   bright   today

the empty blue Aleve bottle

on my work desk

that   I   have   saved   for   thumb-tack   storage

blue   and   yellow

seems   to   smile   at   me

as   sunlight   floods   through   my   office   window

OAKLAND MORNING FOG MINDFULNESS POEM #1

it's   foggy this   morning

a morning for Carl Sandburg

can't   see
the
city

but the cats are out

I worry about the Oakland cats

but they seem to know what they are doing

there is young Mr. Stripes

a   slow moving   black-and-white   Cow Kitty

orange striped Sebastian with the deep meow

and   my   favorite Schwarz

they let   me   pet   them
sometimes

but I   have to   let   them
come
to   me

they don't   like me   calling   *here kitty kitty*

they're city cats
too cool for me

Schwarz   is   watching   me
now

64

sitting on the tallest fence across the   street
only his red eyes
and long tail visible

perhaps he
worries

about   me   too

epileptic   me
sitting   here
alone

in the
dark

this   morning   with   my   American   Spirit

and   my   thoughts

in the Oakland fog

THE APPLE DECORATION

our   Christmas   tree   has   been   abandoned

finished

laying   on   the   street
in front
of   our   house

but   we   laid   it   down   with   respect

it is after all
a tree

but   I   noticed

sitting here
in the morning   fog

that one of Ben's funny red plastic apple   ornaments

has   rolled   onto the
cracked   Oakland
sidewalk

nobody has picked it up
I find this interesting
a little   sad

they   look   very   real

whenever I   forget
to put
them away

they   go   into   a   fruit   bowl

my life is on the street

I go   to   pick   it   up

it's   a   little   beat   up

but   I

put it into
the
fruit
bowl   again

this   makes   me
feel   a bit
better

SELF-DEFINITION MINDFULNESS SONG

I   have   been   called

many things   been   named
in   my   time

sister   lover   daughter
    alcoholic   secretary

and   more

black-sheep   bi-polar   depressed
    schizophrenic

doesn't every writer
have a list?

it's   a   cold   November   morning

I   smoke   on   my   red   clay porch
lit   by   streetlights

ghosts are   calling me   these   names

and   more

but in truth

I've come to be a wise-woman

and a time has come

for   this   to   be   told

knots   untied

no   looking back

over my shoulder

it's   not   strange
that   it   took   me
until 50

to   grow up

stupid   or   wise

I   sit   here   typing

you know I was unable to do this
until   you died
unable   to   define   myself
until   you   were   gone

let's be   honest

you know

you would have talked me out of this

talked me
out
of   this   self-definition
kept me
in your sense of   right for me

so   wrong

this is   partially
my own fault
laziness fear   drinking

but as I said let's be honest

you had me
defined

as   nothing,   ghosts

and I hear you

the simple   thing is   pointing   my finger
the complicated
part

is   the   three   fingers
pointing   back

this   morning   as   I   watch   the
                street   lights
turn

off   as

the   sun   comes   up

trust   me   I   hear   you

but   am   trying

to   listen   only   to   my   own   voice to   the   three   fingers pointing back

saying

wise-woman
wise-woman
wise-woman

BOSCH MINDFULNESS POEM

my grandfather was born in Amsterdam

an immigrant from over
the sea

the only sort-of opera singer from a family

of successful magicians

and actors

he ended up being a subway conductor

in New York City

it's nice to know

that there were other square pegs in the family

I always felt like the only one in a pack
of
perfect nails

he kept a print of *Ship of Fools* by Bosch

on the wall
of the

Brooklyn flat

where my
dad and his little sister grew up
to remind

him not to take another long sea voyage

like the one

he had   been   forced to take to   get   here

my grandma saw   it in   my art history book

pointed it out to me

with her Nuremberg blue eyes

but she   used   German words

to   describe   the   painting

and I think they   describe my   grandfather   too

words   like   *angst*   *weltschmerz*

and
                    lebensmüde

A MOMENT IN OAKLAND TIME # 2

my mom's ghost
sent me

an   Iowa   rainstorm   last   night

complete with   thunder
lights
that lit that sky

just humid enough so I could feel her   kiss

that did the trick

just like she knew it would

I am looking at today with a new light
less grief

new   anticipation

SELF-SABOTAGE MINDFULNESS POEM

how perplexing this is

I just can't
seem to
get   ahead

sitting   here   working
on this poem

instead of my   chapbook

moving   steadily in   the   wrong direction

going   nowhere
real fast

it's easy to do

fall into   a   black   hole

nobody   will   notice

I will still
get   praises

from

my   family   and   friends

simply

for

holding   it   together

Nancy Patrice Davenport is a native of the San Francisco Bay Area currently living in Oakland, California. Her poems are widely published in various journals and anthologies, and have been translated into numerous languages.